pasta
supreme

Published by:
TRIDENT REFERENCE PUBLISHING
801 12th Avenue South, Suite 400
Naples, Fl 34102 USA

Tel: + 1 (239) 649-7077
www.tridentreference.com
email: sales@tridentreference.com

Pasta Supreme
© TRIDENT REFERENCE PUBLISHING

Publisher
Simon St. John Bailey

Editor-in-chief
Susan Knightley

Prepress
Precision Prep & Press

Includes Index
ISBN 1582796602
UPC 6 15269 96602 0

Printed in The United States

introduction

Due to its neutral flavour, pasta always acquires the identity of the sauce on it. Without denying the fact that a good dish of hot spaghetti, dressed with extra virgin olive oil, a bit of butter, salt and pepper can be sublime in its simplicity, in this book we propose different sauces that adapt to the

shape and characteristics of each type of pasta. Since the shape defines the sauce that goes best with it, it is advisable to go over the pasta varieties available to the cook.

- **Penne or penne rigatti** (feathers, plain or striped), and in general all types of tube-shaped pasta, go well with abundant vegetable-based sauces, as they have little absorption surface.
- **Farfalle** (bows or butterflies), dried **gnocchi, shells,** due to their shape and size are fit to hold sauces with minced meat or juicy vegetables like tomatoes or zucchini.
- **Spaghetti, spaghettini, linguine, bucatini,** due to their firm consistency, combine well with shellfish, carbonara or Bolognese sauces, as well as with pesto.
- **Gnocchi** are suitable for creamy sauces and strong cheeses (gorgonzola, roquefort, camembert).

- **Fettuce, fettucine, tagliatelle, pappardelle, nests and all strings** are best with creamy sauces, white sauce and fish.
- **Tortellini, tortelli, cappelletti**, and in general **all filled pasta**, need lighter sauces, that combine with the filling.
- **Lasagna**, filled and baked layers of pasta, require fairly liquid sauces that can be absorbed by the dough as it cooks.
- **Angel hair** can be used for stir-fries in a wok or for other Oriental specialties.

Pasta leftovers

- They can be mixed with white sauce, sprinkled with cheese and heated under the oven grill.
- Another option is to use them to make a Spanish omelette.
- Combined with avocados, cherry tomatoes, shrimps, a few drops of olive oil, lemon juice, salt and pepper, they can be turned into a delicious salad.
- Bound together with a mixture of egg and flour, they are useful for making fritters.

Difficulty scale

■□□ I Easy to do

■■□ I Requires attention

■■■ I Requires experience

tomato
and basil pasta bake

■□□ | Cooking time: 30 minutes - Preparation time: 20 minutes

method

1. Place hot pasta and 125 g/4 oz cheese in a lightly greased ovenproof dish, mix to combine and set aside.

2. Cook ham in a nonstick frying pan for 3-4 minutes. Add mushrooms and cook for 3 minutes longer. Spoon ham mixture over pasta and top with pasta sauce and basil. Combine breadcrumbs and remaining cheese. Sprinkle cheese mixture over pasta and bake at 200°C/400°F/Gas 6 for 20 minutes.

ingredients

> **500 g/1 lb pasta of your choice, cooked**
> **220 g/7 oz tasty cheese (mature Cheddar), grated**
> **8 slices ham, shredded**
> **250 g/8 oz button mushrooms, sliced**
> **750 g/1 1/2 lb jar tomato pasta sauce**
> **2 tablespoons chopped fresh basil**
> **30 g/1 oz breadcrumbs, made from stale bread**

....
Serves 4

tip from the chef

Accompany with a broccoli and cauliflower salad. To make salad, combine 2 tablespoons lemon juice, 2 teaspoons Dijon mustard, 3 tablespoons olive oil, 1 tablespoon finely chopped fresh parsley and black pepper to taste and toss with cooked broccoli and cauliflower florets.

penne
napolitana

a

■□□ | Cooking time: 30 minutes - Preparation time: 20 minutes

method

1. Cook pasta in boiling water in a large saucepan following packet directions. Drain, set aside and keep warm.
2. To make sauce, heat oil in a saucepan over a medium heat. Add onions and garlic and cook, stirring (a), for 3 minutes or until onions are soft.
3. Stir in tomatoes, wine (b), parsley, oregano (c) and black pepper to taste, bring to simmering and simmer for 15 minutes or until sauce reduces and thickens.
4. To serve, spoon sauce over hot pasta (d) and top with shavings of Parmesan cheese.

....
Serves 4

ingredients

> **500 g/1 lb penne**
> **fresh Parmesan cheese**

napolitana sauce

> **2 teaspoons olive oil**
> **2 onions, chopped**
> **2 cloves garlic, crushed**
> **2 x 440 g/14 oz canned tomatoes, undrained and mashed**
> **3/4 cup/185 ml/6 fl oz red wine**
> **1 tablespoon chopped flat-leaf parsley**
> **1 tablespoon chopped fresh oregano or 1/2 teaspoon dried oregano**
> **freshly ground black pepper**

tip from the chef

Penne is a short tubular pasta similar to macaroni, but with the ends cut at an angle rather than straight. If penne are unavailable, macaroni are a suitable alternative for this recipe.

b

c

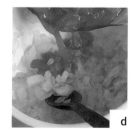
d

pasta
putanesca

■□□ I Cooking time: 5 minutes - Preparation time: 20 minutes

method

1. Cook pasta in boiling water in a large saucepan following packet directions. Drain, set aside and keep warm.

2. To make sauce, heat oil in a saucepan over a low heat, add garlic and cook, stirring, for 2 minutes. Add tomatoes and bring to the boil, then stir in anchovies, black olives, capers, oregano and chili powder and simmer for 3 minutes longer. Spoon sauce over hot pasta, sprinkle with parsley and Parmesan cheese and serve.

....
Serves 6

ingredients

> 500 g/1 lb linguine or thin spaghetti

putanesca sauce
> 2 tablespoons olive oil
> 5 cloves garlic, crushed
> 4 x 440 g/14 oz canned peeled Italian plum tomatoes, drained and chopped
> 6 anchovy fillets, coarsely chopped
> 60 g/2 oz stoned black olives
> 2 tablespoons capers, drained and chopped
> 1 teaspoon dried oregano
> 1/4 teaspoon chili powder
> 1/2 bunch parsley, coarsely chopped
> 30 g/1 oz grated Parmesan cheese

tip from the chef
The reserved juice from the tomatoes can be frozen and used in a casserole or soup at a later date.

spaghetti
bolognese

■□□ | Cooking time: 25 minutes - Preparation time: 20 minutes

method

1. To make sauce, heat oil in a frying pan over a medium heat. Add garlic and onion and cook, stirring (a), for 3 minutes or until onion is soft.
2. Add beef and cook, stirring (b), for 5 minutes or until meat is well browned. Stir in tomato purée (passata), wine or water (c), oregano and thyme. Bring to simmering and simmer, stirring occasionally, for 15 minutes or until sauce reduces and thickens. Season to taste with black pepper.
3. Cook pasta in boiling water in a large saucepan following packet directions. Drain well. To serve, spoon sauce over hot pasta and top with Parmesan cheese, if using.

....
Serves 4

ingredients

> 500 g/1 lb spaghetti
> grated Parmesan cheese (optional)

bolognese sauce

> 2 teaspoons vegetable oil
> 1 clove garlic, crushed
> 1 onion, chopped
> 500 g/1 lb beef mince
> 440 g/14 oz canned tomato purée (passata)
> 1/4 cup/60 ml/2 fl oz red wine or water
> 1 tablespoon chopped fresh oregano or 1/2 teaspoon dried oregano
> 1 tablespoon chopped fresh thyme or 1/2 teaspoon dried thyme
> freshly ground black pepper

tip from the chef

For an easy family meal serve this all-time favorite with steamed vegetables or a tossed green salad and crusty bread or rolls.

a

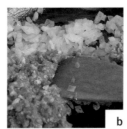
b

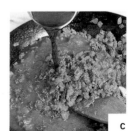
c

fettuccine pesto

■□□ | Cooking time: 10 minutes - Preparation time: 10 minutes

method

1. Cook pasta in boiling water in a large saucepan following packet directions. Drain, set aside and keep warm.
2. To make pesto, place Parmesan cheese, garlic, pine nuts and basil in a food processor or blender and process to finely chop. With machine running, gradually add oil and continue processing to form a smooth paste. To serve, spoon pesto over hot pasta and toss to combine.

Serves 4

ingredients

> **500 g/1 lb fettuccine**

basil pesto

> **100 g/3½ oz fresh Parmesan cheese, chopped**
> **2 cloves garlic, crushed**
> **60 g/2 oz pine nuts**
> **1 large bunch basil, leaves removed and stems discarded**
> **¼ cup/60 ml/2 fl oz olive oil**

tip from the chef

Basil is one of the herbs that characterizes Italian cooking. This pesto can be made when basil is plentiful, then frozen and used as required. Treat yourself to this dish in mid-winter to remind you of balmy summer days.

vegetable
pasta salad

■☐☐ | Cooking time: 20 minutes - Preparation time: 20 minutes

ingredients

> **500 g/1 lb small pasta shapes of your choice**
> **250 g/8 oz broccoli, broken into florets**
> **250 g/8 oz cherry tomatoes, halved**
> **6 spring onions, cut into 2.5 cm/1 in lengths**
> **12 black olives**

red wine dressing

> **2 tablespoons red wine vinegar**
> **1/2 cup/125 ml/4fl oz olive oil**
> **2 tablespoons grated fresh Parmesan cheese**
> **1 clove garlic, crushed**
> **freshly ground black pepper**

method

1. Cook pasta in boiling water in a large saucepan, following packet directions. Drain, rinse under cold running water, then drain again and set aside to cool completely.
2. Boil, steam or microwave broccoli for 2-3 minutes or until it just changes color. Refresh under cold running water. Drain, then dry on absorbent kitchen paper.
3. To make dressing, place vinegar, oil, Parmesan cheese, garlic and black pepper to taste in a screw-top jar and shake to combine.
4. Place pasta, broccoli, tomatoes, spring onions and olives in a salad bowl. Pour dressing over and toss to combine.

....
Serves 8

tip from the chef
All greens and vegetables go well with pasta and enhance its flavor.

pasta with
six herb sauce

■□□ | Cooking time: 15 minutes - Preparation time: 5 minutes

method

1. Cook pasta in boiling water in a large saucepan following packet directions. Drain, set aside and keep warm.
2. To make sauce, melt butter in a saucepan over a medium heat. Add rosemary, sage, basil, marjoram, oregano, parsley and garlic and cook, stirring, for 1 minute.
3. Stir in wine and stock, bring to simmering and simmer for 4 minutes. To serve, spoon sauce over hot pasta and toss to combine.

Serves 4

ingredients

> **500 g/1 lb pasta shapes of your choice**

six herb sauce
> **30 g/1 oz butter**
> **2 tablespoons chopped fresh rosemary**
> **12 small fresh sage leaves**
> **12 small fresh basil leaves**
> **2 tablespoons fresh marjoram leaves**
> **2 tablespoons fresh oregano leaves**
> **2 tablespoons chopped fresh parsley**
> **2 cloves garlic, chopped**
> **1/4 cup/60 ml/2 fl oz white wine**
> **1/4 cup/60 ml/2 fl oz vegetable stock**

tip from the chef

Equally delicious as a light meal or as the first course of a dinner party, this dish must be made using fresh, not dried, herbs. However, the herbs can be changed according to what is available. If you can only get four of the herbs then just use those.

fettuccine
with coriander sauce

■□□ | Cooking time: 10 minutes - Preparation time: 10 minutes

ingredients
> **500 g/1 lb fettuccine**

coriander sauce
> **2 cloves garlic, chopped**
> **60 g/2 oz walnut pieces**
> **60 g/2 oz coriander leaves**
> **15 g/1/2 oz fresh parsley leaves**
> **4 tablespoons vegetable oil**
> **60 g/2 oz grated Parmesan cheese**
> **freshly ground black pepper**

method
1. Cook fettuccine in boiling water in a large saucepan following packet directions. Drain, set aside and keep warm.
2. To make sauce, place garlic, walnuts, coriander and parsley in a food processor or blender and process to finely chop. With machine running, add oil in a steady stream. Add Parmesan cheese and black pepper to taste, and process to combine.
3. Spoon sauce over pasta and toss to combine. Serve immediately.

....
Serves 6

tip from the chef
If a milder flavor is preferred, replace coriander by fresh parsley.

fettuccine
with leeks

■□□ | Cooking time: 25 minutes - Preparation time: 15 minutes

method

1. Cook fettuccine in boiling water in a large saucepan following packet directions. Drain, set aside and keep warm.
2. Heat butter in a large frying pan and cook leeks for 8-10 minutes or until tender. Add ham and red pepper and cook for 2-3 minutes longer. Stir in cream, bring to the boil, then reduce heat and simmer for 4-5 minutes.
3. Add fettuccine to pan and toss to combine. Season with black pepper (to taste) and serve immediately.

ingredients

- > 500 g/1 lb fettuccine
- > 60 g/2 oz butter
- > 2 large leeks, halved and thinly sliced
- > 185 g/6 oz ham, cut into strips
- > 1 red pepper, cut into strips
- > 1 cup/250 ml/8 fl oz thickened (double) cream
- > freshly ground black pepper

....
Serves 4

tip from the chef

Leeks, spring onions, garlic, chives, shallots, all liliaceous plants are an excellent seasoning for pasta.

hot sun-dried tomato pasta

■□□ | Cooking time: 15 minutes - Preparation time: 10 minutes

ingredients

> **¹/₂ bunch spring onions**
> **250 g/1 lb bow pasta**
> **1 teaspoon butter**
> **1 tablespoon olive oil**
> **1 small chili, seeded and sliced**
> **2 tablespoons brandy**
> **300 ml/10 fl oz cream**
> **¹/₃ cup sun-dried tomatoes**
> **freshly ground black pepper**

method

1. Wash and trim spring onions. Slice into 2 cm/³/₄ in lengths. Place pasta in boiling water and cook until al dente. Drain, and place in warm serving bowl.
2. Heat butter and oil in frying pan, sauté onions and chili for 1 minute. Add brandy, cream and sliced sun-dried tomatoes. Simmer until sauce thickens. Season with pepper.
3. Pour over pasta. Serve with Parmesan cheese and sprinkle with freshly ground black pepper to taste.

....
Serves 4

tip from the chef
Brandy can be replaced by a late harvest white wine, like the French Sauternes.

vegetable
and chili pasta

a

b

■□□ | Cooking time: 25 minutes - Preparation time: 20 minutes

method

1. Cut eggplant into 2 cm/3/4 in cubes. Place in a colander, sprinkle with salt and set aside to drain for 10 minutes. Rinse eggplant under cold running water and pat dry.

2. Cook pasta in boiling water in a large saucepan, following packet directions. Drain, set aside and keep warm.

3. Heat oil in a large frying pan over a medium heat and cook eggplant (a) in batches, for 5 minutes or until golden. Remove eggplant from pan, drain on absorbent kitchen paper and set aside.

4. Add onions, chilies and garlic to pan and cook, stirring (b), for 3 minutes or until onions are golden. Return eggplant to pan (c). Stir in tomatoes, wine (d) and basil, bring to a simmer and cook for 5 minutes (e). To serve, spoon sauce over hot pasta.

....
Serves 4

ingredients

> **2 eggplant**
> **salt**
> **500 g/1 lb pasta shells**
> **1/4 cup/60 ml/2 fl oz olive oil**
> **2 onions, chopped**
> **2 fresh red chilies, seeded and chopped**
> **2 cloves garlic, crushed**
> **2 x 440 g/14 oz canned tomatoes, undrained and mashed**
> **1/2 cup/125 ml/4 fl oz dry white wine**
> **2 tablespoons chopped fresh basil or 1 teaspoon dried basil**

tip from the chef

The combination of eggplant, tomato and goat cheese is a good flavoring for pasta.

c

d

e

pasta
and vegetable stir-fry

■□□ | Cooking time: 16 minutes - Preparation time: 30 minutes

ingredients
> **30 g/1 oz dried Chinese mushrooms**
> **315 g/10 oz large fusilli pasta (spirals or twists)**
> **3 tablespoons vegetable oil**
> **60 g/2 oz raw cashews**
> **2 cloves garlic, crushed**
> **1 teaspoon finely grated fresh ginger**
> **315 g/10 oz Chinese cabbage, sliced**
> **90 g/3 oz snow peas**
> **6 spring onions, sliced diagonally**
> **3 tablespoons Chinese rice wine**
> **2 tablespoons light soy sauce**
> **1 tablespoon sweet chili sauce**

method
1. Place mushrooms in a bowl, cover with boiling water and soak for 10 minutes or until mushrooms are tender. Drain, remove stems and cut mushrooms into thin strips.
2. Cook pasta in boiling water in a large saucepan, following packet directions. Drain, set aside and keep warm.
3. Heat 1 tablespoon oil in a wok over a medium heat, add cashews and stir-fry for 1-2 minutes or until golden. Remove from pan and drain on absorbent kitchen paper.
4. Heat remaining oil in pan, add garlic and ginger and stir-fry for 1 minute. Add cabbage, snow peas, spring onions and mushrooms and stir-fry for 2-3 minutes or until vegetables change color. Stir in rice wine, soy sauce and chili sauce, bring to simmering and simmer for 1 minute. Add cashews and pasta and toss to combine.

....
Serves 4

tip from the chef
Look for Chinese mushrooms at Oriental food stores and at greengrocers. If unavailable, substitute with any fresh mushroom of your choice, or use a combination of mushrooms.

forest
mushroom pasta

■□□ | Cooking time: 20 minutes - Preparation time: 10 minutes

method

1. Cook pasta in boiling water in a large saucepan following packet directions. Drain, set aside and keep warm.
2. To make sauce, melt butter in a saucepan over a medium heat. Stir in flour and cook, stirring, for 1 minute. Remove pan from heat and whisk in milk. Return pan to heat and cook, stirring, until sauce boils and thickens. Stir in nutmeg and season to taste with black pepper. Add sauce to pasta and mix to combine. Set aside and keep warm.
3. Heat oil in a frying pan over a medium heat. Add garlic and mushrooms and cook, stirring, for 4 minutes or until mushrooms are soft. To serve, top pasta with mushroom mixture.

ingredients

> **375 g/12 oz pasta of your choice**
> **2 teaspoons vegetable oil**
> **1 clove garlic, crushed**
> **750 g/1 1/2 lb mixed mushrooms**

white sauce

> **30 g/1 oz butter**
> **2 tablespoons flour**
> **2 cups/500 ml/16 fl oz milk**
> **1/2 teaspoon ground nutmeg**
> **freshly ground black pepper**

....

Serves 4

tip from the chef

If you can only get ordinary mushrooms, add a few dried mushrooms for extra flavor. You will need to soak the dried mushrooms in boiling water for 20 minutes or until they are soft. Drain well, then slice or chop and add to the fresh mushrooms when cooking. Dried mushrooms have a strong flavor, so you only need to add a few.

cappellini
with tomatoes

■□□ | Cooking time: 15 minutes - Preparation time: 10 minutes

ingredients
> 120 ml/4 fl oz olive oil
> 6 cloves garlic, thinly sliced
> 550 g/17 oz Roma tomatoes, seeded and diced
> 1/3 cup fresh basil, shredded
> salt
> freshly ground black pepper
> 400 g/13 oz cappellini

method
1. Heat 60 ml/2 oz of the oil in a pan, add the garlic, and cook over a medium heat until garlic is slightly browned and golden.
2. Reduce the heat, then add the tomatoes, basil, salt and pepper, and cook for 5 minutes or until tomatoes are just heated through.
3. Cook cappellini pasta in boiling salted water until al dente. Add remaining oil.
4. Serve with tomato mixture over cappellini pasta.

....
Serves 4-6

tip from the chef
To peel tomatoes easily, make a small slit on the base and cover with boiling water for a few minutes. Drain, allow to cool a little and peel.

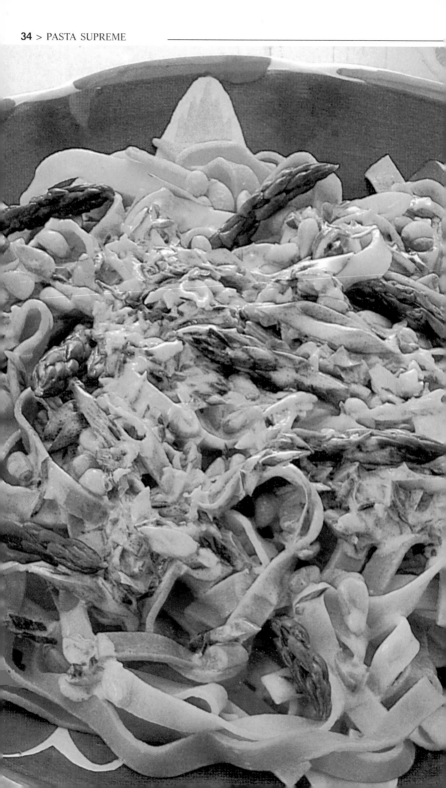

asparagus
fettuccine

■■□ | Cooking time: 17 minutes - Preparation time: 30 minutes

method

1. Cook pasta in boiling water in a large saucepan following packet directions. Drain, set aside and keep warm.
2. To make sauce, melt butter in a saucepan over a medium heat, add spring onions and garlic and cook, stirring, for 2 minutes or until onions are soft.
3. Stir in cream, bring to simmering and simmer for 3 minutes. Stir in asparagus and cook for 2 minutes longer. Add pine nuts and black pepper to taste. Spoon sauce over pasta and toss to combine. Serve immediately.

Serves 4

ingredients

> **500 g/1 lb fresh fettuccine**

creamy asparagus sauce
> **15 g/^{1}/$_2$ oz butter**
> **6 spring onions, sliced**
> **1 clove garlic, crushed**
> **2 cups/500 ml/16 fl oz cream (double)**
> **375 g/12 oz asparagus, blanched and cut into 2.5 cm/1 in pieces**
> **60 g/2 oz pine nuts, toasted**
> **freshly ground black pepper**

tip from the chef

Fresh or packaged dried pasta? Which is the best? Neither is superior – they are just different. Fresh pasta is more delicate and keeps for only a few days, while dried pasta is more stable and ideal for serving with heartier sauces and to have on hand as a store cupboard ingredient.

fettuccine
carbonara

a

■□□ | Cooking time: 15 minutes - Preparation time: 10 minutes

method

1. Cook pasta in boiling water in a large saucepan following packet directions. Drain, set aside and keep warm.
2. To make sauce, cook ham, prosciutto or bacon in a frying pan (a) over a medium heat for 3 minutes or until crisp.
3. Stir in stock (b) and cream (c), bring to simmering and simmer until sauce is reduced by half.
4. Remove pan from heat, whisk in eggs (d), parsley and black pepper to taste. Return pan to heat and cook, stirring, for 1 minute. Remove pan from heat, add hot pasta to sauce and toss to combine. Serve immediately.

ingredients

> 500 g/1 lb fettuccine

carbonara sauce

> 250 g/8 oz ham, prosciutto or bacon, chopped
> 1/2 cup/125 ml/4 fl oz chicken stock
> 1 cup/250 ml/8 fl oz cream (double)
> 7 eggs, lightly beaten
> 2 tablespoons chopped flat-leaf parsley
> freshly ground black pepper

....
Serves 6

tip from the chef

Carbonara is a succulent, classical sauce. For a lighter version, it can be made without cream, with fewer eggs and using prosciutto ham instead of bacon.

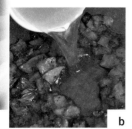
b

c

d

fettuccine
with bacon and cream

■□□ I Cooking time: 12 minutes - Preparation time: 5 minutes

ingredients

> **500 g/1 lb dried fettuccine**
> **4 tablespoons grated Parmesan cheese**

bacon and cream sauce

> **2 rashers of bacon, trimmed and chopped**
> **4 green shallots, chopped**
> **1/2 cup/125 ml/4 fl oz cream**
> **1/2 cup/125 ml/4 fl oz chicken stock**
> **3 tablespoons chopped sun-dried tomatoes (optional)**

method

1. Cook fettuccine in boiling water in a large saucepan following packet directions. Drain and set aside to keep warm.
2. To make sauce, cook bacon in a large frying pan for 4-5 minutes or until crisp. Add shallots, and cook for 1 minute longer. Stir in cream and stock, bring to the boil then reduce heat and simmer until reduced and thickened. Stir in sun-dried tomatoes and toss fettuccine in cream sauce. Sprinkle with Parmesan cheese and serve.

....
Serves 4

tip from the chef

A crisp salad and crusty bread is all that is needed to complete this course.

gnocchi
with gorgonzola sauce

■□□ | Cooking time: 15 minutes - Preparation time: 10 minutes

method

1. Cook gnocchi in boiling water in a large saucepan following packet directions. Drain, set aside and keep warm.

2. To make sauce, place gorgonzola or blue cheese, milk and butter in a saucepan and cook over a low heat, stirring, for 4-5 minutes or until cheese melts. Stir in walnuts, cream and black pepper to taste, bring to simmering and simmer for 5 minutes or until sauce reduces and thickens. Spoon sauce over hot gnocchi and toss to combine.

Serves 6

ingredients

> **500 g/1 lb potato gnocchi**

gorgonzola sauce

> **200 g/6 1/2 oz gorgonzola or blue cheese, crumbled**
> **3/4 cup/185 ml/6 fl oz milk**
> **60 g/2 oz butter**
> **60 g/2 oz walnuts, toasted and chopped**
> **200 ml/6 1/2 fl oz cream (double)**
> **freshly ground black pepper**

tip from the chef

Potato gnocchi are available from specialty pasta shops. This sauce is also great with shell pasta, penne, macaroni, tortellini or farfalle.

farfalle
with whisky sauce

■□□ | Cooking time: 15 minutes - Preparation time: 20 minutes

ingredients
> 375 g/12 oz farfalle

whisky and peppercorn sauce
> 15 g/1/2 oz butter
> 125 g/4 oz button mushrooms, sliced
> 4 spring onions, sliced
> 1 1/4 cups/315 g/10 oz sour cream
> 2 teaspoons French mustard
> 2 teaspoons crushed green peppercorns
> 1/4 cup/60 ml/2 fl oz vegetable stock
> 1 tablespoon whisky

method
1. Cook pasta in boiling water in a large saucepan following packet directions. Drain, set aside and keep warm.
2. To make sauce, melt butter in a frying pan over a medium heat, add mushrooms and spring onions and cook, stirring, for 2-3 minutes or until mushrooms are soft.
3. Stir in sour cream, mustard, peppercorns, stock and whisky, bring to simmering and simmer for 1 minute. Spoon sauce over pasta and toss gently to combine.

....
Serves 4

tip from the chef
Farfalle means butterflies and this is what this pretty bow-shaped pasta looks like.

raspberry
salmon pasta

a

■□□ | Cooking time: 17 minutes - Preparation time: 15 minutes

method

1. To make mayonnaise, place raspberries in a food processor or blender and process until smooth. Push purée through a fine sieve and discard seeds. Add mayonnaise, mustard and lemon juice to purée, mix to combine and set aside.

2. Cook pasta in boiling water in a large saucepan, following packet directions. Drain, set aside and keep warm.

3. Heat oil in a frying or grill pan over a medium heat. Brush salmon with lemon juice (a) and sprinkle with dill. Place salmon in pan and cook for 2-3 minutes each side (b) or until flesh flakes when tested with a fork. Remove salmon from pan and cut into thick slices (c).

4. To serve, divide pasta between six serving plates. Top with salmon slices and drizzle with raspberry mayonnaise. Serve immediately.

ingredients

> **500 g/1 lb pepper or plain fettuccine**
> **1 tablespoon vegetable oil**
> **500 g/1 lb salmon fillet, bones and skin removed**
> **2 tablespoons lemon juice**
> **2 tablespoons chopped fresh dill**

raspberry mayonnaise

> **200 g/6¹/₂ oz raspberries**
> **1 cup/250 g/8 oz mayonnaise**
> **2 teaspoons wholegrain mustard**
> **1 tablespoon lemon juice**

....
Serves 6

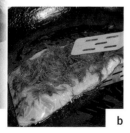

b

c

tip from the chef
For variation, cream can be used instead of mayonnaise.

quick
fettuccine with scallops

■□□ | Cooking time: 20 minutes - Preparation time: 10 minutes

ingredients

> 500 g/1 lb fettuccine

scallop sauce

> 30 g/1 oz butter
> 1 red pepper, cut into strips
> 2 spring onions, finely chopped
> 1 cup/250 ml/8 fl oz thickened cream (double)
> 500 g/1 lb scallops
> freshly ground black pepper
> 1 tablespoon finely chopped fresh parsley

method

1. Cook fettuccine in boiling water in a large saucepan, following packet directions. Drain, set aside and keep warm.

2. To make sauce, melt butter in a large frying pan and cook red pepper and spring onions for 1-2 minutes. Add cream and bring to the boil, then reduce heat and simmer for 5 minutes or until sauce reduces slightly and thickens.

3. Stir scallops into sauce and cook for 2-3 minutes or until scallops are opaque. Season to taste with black pepper. Place fettuccine in a warm serving bowl, top with sauce and sprinkle with parsley.

....

Serves 4

tip from the chef

When pasta with sauce is left over, it can be reconditioned by adding milk and sprinkling cheese on it, and then baking until golden.

tuna-filled shells

■ □ □ | Cooking time: 15 minutes - Preparation time: 25 minutes

method

1. Cook 8 pasta shells in a large saucepan of boiling water until al dente. Drain, rinse under cold running water and drain again. Set aside, then repeat with remaining shells; ensure cooked shells do not overlap.

2. To make filling, place ricotta cheese and tuna in a bowl and mix to combine. Mix in red pepper, capers, chives and 2 tablespoons grated Swiss cheese, nutmeg and black pepper to taste.

3. Fill each shell with ricotta mixture, and place in a lightly greased, shallow ovenproof dish. Sprinkle with Parmesan cheese and remaining Swiss cheese. Place under a preheated grill and cook until cheese melts.

....
Makes 16

ingredients

> **16 giant pasta shells**

tuna filling

> **250 g/8 oz ricotta cheese, drained**
> **440 g/14 oz canned tuna in brine, drained and flaked**
> **1/2 red pepper, diced**
> **1 tablespoon chopped capers**
> **1 teaspoon snipped fresh chives**
> **4 tablespoons grated Swiss cheese**
> **pinch ground nutmeg**
> **freshly ground black pepper**
> **2 tablespoons grated fresh Parmesan cheese**

tip from the chef

This tuna mixture, without ricotta cheese, can also be used as a sauce for ravioli, agnolotti or any pasta stuffed with ricotta cheese.

lobster
in pasta nets

■ ■ ■ | Cooking time: 20 minutes - Preparation time: 45 minutes

ingredients

> **375 g/12 oz angel hair pasta**
> **3 uncooked lobster tails, shelled and flesh cut into 4 cm/1¹/2 in pieces**
> **flour**
> **vegetable oil for deep frying**

lime cream

> **¹/2 cup/125 g/4 oz mayonnaise**
> **¹/4 cup/60 g/2 oz sour cream**
> **1 tablespoon finely grated lime rind**
> **1 tablespoon lime juice**
> **1 tablespoon wholegrain mustard**
> **2 tablespoons chopped fresh tarragon or 1 teaspoon dried tarragon**

method

1. Cook pasta in boiling water in a large saucepan until almost cooked. Drain, rinse under cold running water, drain again and pat dry on absorbent kitchen paper (a). Set aside.
2. To make lime cream, place mayonnaise, sour cream, lime rind, lime juice, mustard and tarragon in a bowl and mix to combine. Set aside.
3. Dust lobster pieces with flour. Wrap a few stands of pasta around each lobster piece (b). Continue wrapping with pasta to form a net effect around lobster.
4. Heat oil in a large saucepan until a cube of bread dropped in browns in 50 seconds. Cook pasta-wrapped lobster in batches for 2-3 minutes or until golden (c). Drain on absorbent kitchen paper and serve immediately with lime cream.

....
Serves 4

tip from the chef

This dish is also delicious made with large uncooked prawns.

a

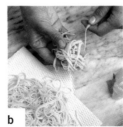

b

c

tagliatelle
with chili octopus

■ ■ □ | Cooking time: 22 minutes - Preparation time: 15 minutes

method

1. To make marinade, place sesame oil, ginger, lime juice and chili sauce in a large bowl and mix to combine. Add octopus, toss to coat, cover and marinate in the refrigerator for 3-4 hours.
2. Cook pasta in boiling water in a large saucepan following packet directions. Drain, set aside and keep warm.
3. To make sauce, heat oil in a saucepan over a medium heat. Add spring onions and cook, stirring, for 1 minute. Stir in tomato purée (passata), bring to simmering and simmer for 4 minutes.
4. Cook octopus under a preheated hot grill for 5-7 minutes or until tender. Add octopus to sauce and toss to combine. Spoon octopus mixture over hot pasta and toss to combine.

ingredients

> 1 kg/2 lb baby octopus, cleaned
> 500 g/1 lb spinach tagliatelle

chili ginger marinade

> 1 tablespoon sesame oil
> 1 tablespoon grated fresh ginger
> 2 tablespoons lime juice
> 2 tablespoons sweet chili sauce

tomato sauce

> 2 teaspoons vegetable oil
> 3 spring onions, sliced diagonally
> 440 g/14 oz canned tomato purée (passata)

....
Serves 4

tip from the chef

As a main course, all this dish needs is a sauté of mixed vegetables or a tossed green salad and crusty bread or rolls. If served on its own as a starter, it will serve six. This is also delicious made with squid rings instead of octopus.

scallop and
pepper pasta

■■□ | Cooking time: 30 minutes - Preparation time: 15 minutes

ingredients

- > 500 g/1 lb tagliarini
- > 1 tablespoon olive oil
- > 500 g/1 lb scallops
- > 100 g/3¹/2 oz prosciutto or lean ham, cut into thin strips
- > 2 tablespoons lemon juice
- > 2 tablespoons chopped fresh basil or 1 teaspoon dried basil
- > freshly ground black pepper
- > 1 cup/250 ml/8 fl oz chicken stock
- > 1 red pepper, cut into strips
- > 2 leeks, cut into strips

gremolata

- > 3 cloves garlic, crushed
- > ¹/2 bunch flat-leaf parsley, leaves finely chopped
- > 1 tablespoon finely grated lemon rind

method

1. To make gremolata, place garlic, parsley and lemon rind in a bowl and mix well to combine.
2. Cook pasta in boiling water in a large saucepan, following packet directions. Drain, set aside and keep warm.
3. Heat oil in a frying pan over a medium heat. Add scallops and prosciutto or ham and cook, stirring, for 3 minutes or until scallops just turn opaque and prosciutto or ham is crisp. Remove pan from heat, stir in lemon juice, basil and black pepper to taste and set aside.
4. Place stock in a saucepan, bring to a simmer and cook until reduced by half. Add red pepper and leeks and simmer for 3 minutes. Add pasta and scallop mixture to stock mixture. Toss to combine and top with gremolata.

....
Serves 4

tip from the chef

When pepper is used to season pasta, it must always be fresh, ground in a wooden pepper mill and served at once.

tortellini
with onion confit

■ ■ □ | Cooking time: 45 minutes - Preparation time: 5 minutes

method

1. To make confit, melt butter in a saucepan over a medium heat, add onions (a) and cook, stirring, for 3 minutes or until onions are soft. Stir in sugar (b) and cook for 2 minutes longer. Add thyme, wine and vinegar (c), bring to simmering and simmer, stirring frequently, for 40 minutes or until mixture reduces and thickens.

2. Place stock in a saucepan, bring to the boil and boil until reduced by half. Keep warm.

3. Cook pasta in boiling water in a large saucepan following packet directions. Drain well. Add pasta, confit, peas and tarragon to stock, bring to simmering and simmer for 2-3 minutes or until peas are just cooked.

....

Serves 4

ingredients

> 1 1/2 cups/375 ml/ 12 fl oz beef stock
> 750 g/1 1/2 lb beef or veal tortellini
> 250 g/8 oz small peas
> 2 tablespoons chopped fresh tarragon or 1 teaspoon dried tarragon

onion confit

> 30 g/1 oz butter
> 2 onions, thinly sliced
> 2 teaspoons sugar
> 1 tablespoon chopped fresh thyme or 1/2 teaspoon dried thyme
> 1 cup/250 ml/8 fl oz red wine
> 2 tablespoons red wine vinegar

tip from the chef

Serve this unusual pasta dish with a sauté of mixed green vegetables and crusty bread or rolls.

a

b

c

tortellini
with avocado cream

■□□ | Cooking time: 5 minutes - Preparation time: 10 minutes

method

1. Cook tortellini in boiling water in a large saucepan following packet directions. Drain, set aside and keep warm.
2. To make avocado cream, place avocado, cream, Parmesan cheese and lemon juice in a food processor or blender and process until smooth. Season to taste with black pepper.
3. Place tortellini in a warm serving bowl, add avocado cream and toss to combine. Serve immediately.

....
Serves 4

ingredients

> **500 g/1 lb tortellini**

avocado cream

> **1/2 ripe avocado, stoned and peeled**
> **1/4 cup/60 ml/2 fl oz cream (double)**
> **30 g/1 oz grated fresh Parmesan cheese**
> **1 teaspoon lemon juice**
> **freshly ground black pepper**

tip from the chef

Avocado can be replaced by cooked, processed zucchini. The sauce should be very hot to avoid cooling down the pasta.

ravioli
with lemon sauce

■□□ | Cooking time: 10 minutes - Preparation time: 10 minutes

ingredients

> 500 g/1 lb cheese and spinach ravioli
> 30 g/1 oz slivered almonds, toasted

lemon cream sauce

> 30 g/1 oz butter
> 1 clove garlic, crushed
> 1¹/4 cups/315 ml/10 fl oz cream (double)
> ¹/4 cup/60 ml/2 fl oz lemon juice
> 30 g/1 oz grated fresh Parmesan cheese
> 3 tablespoons snipped fresh chives
> 1 teaspoon finely grated lemon rind
> 2 tablespoons chopped fresh parsley
> freshly ground black pepper

method

1. Cook pasta in boiling water in a large saucepan following packet directions. Drain, set aside and keep warm.
2. To make sauce, melt butter in a frying pan over a low heat, add garlic and cook, stirring, for 1 minute. Stir in cream, lemon juice, Parmesan cheese, chives and lemon rind, bring to simmering and simmer for 2 minutes. Add parsley and black pepper to taste and cook for 1 minute longer. Spoon sauce over pasta and toss to combine. Scatter with almonds and serve.

....
Serves 4

tip from the chef

Equally delicious made with cheese and spinach agnolotti (crescent or half-moon shaped ravioli) or tortellini.

ravioli
with walnut sauce

◼◻◻ | Cooking time: 5 minutes - Preparation time: 10 minutes

method

1. Cook ravioli in boiling water in a large saucepan following packet directions. Drain, set aside and keep warm.
2. To make sauce, place walnuts and basil in a food processor or blender and process until finely chopped. Add butter, Parmesan cheese and black pepper to taste. With machine still running, slowly add oil and cream and process until it is just combined. To serve, spoon sauce over pasta and toss.

....
Serves 4

ingredients

> **750 g/1¹/₂ lb cheese and spinach ravioli**

walnut sauce

> **200 g/6¹/₂ oz walnuts**
> **¹/₂ bunch fresh basil, leaves removed and stems discarded**
> **45 g/1¹/₂ oz butter, softened**
> **45 g/1¹/₂ oz grated Parmesan cheese**
> **freshly ground black pepper**
> **100 ml/3¹/₂ fl oz olive oil**
> **155 ml/5 fl oz cream (double)**

tip from the chef

Take care when making the sauce. Only process it briefly or until the ingredients are just combined once the cream is added. If you overprocess, the cream may separate and cause the sauce to curdle.

index